Jean-François Kieffer
Christine Ponsard

Translated by Janet Chevrier

The Illustrated
Gospel

for Children

Ignatius

MAGNIFICAT.

Original French edition:
L'Évangile pour les enfants en bandes dessinées

© 2002 by Fleurus Mame, Paris
© 2010 by Ignatius Press, San Francisco · Magnificat USA LLC, New York
All rights reserved
ISBN Ignatius Press 978-1-58617-511-5 · ISBN Magnificat 978-1-936260-11-9
Library of Congress Control Number 010927109

Printed by Tien Wah Press, Malaysia
Printed on July 17, 2010
Job Number MGN 10006

TABLE OF CONTENTS

No one has ever seen God, not you, not me. No one. Yet the Good News, this Gospel of Jesus Christ, has echoed through the ages for two thousand years: God became man!

Jesus speaks and God speaks in the words of man. Jesus acts and God acts like man. Jesus loves and God loves with the heart of man. The Father loved you so much that he sent his Son, Jesus, so that you could know him. And to know Jesus is to have eternal life. You live in your home, you go to school, you play, you sleep: in every moment of your life, if you know Jesus, you "dwell" in him and he dwells in you. He lives with you; he is with you when you pray and when you sleep.

So you speak like Jesus, like God. You act like Jesus, like God. You love like Jesus, like God.

If you love Jesus, you will love your parents, your brothers, your sisters, and your friends. I am sure this book will help you to know Jesus, to love him, to speak to him, to listen to him. And then you will live in joy and in peace.

Jean Villeminot

THE ANNUNCIATION

Luke 1:26–38

Anne and Joachim have a little girl named Mary.

She is full of the love and joy of God.

Mary grows up and waits for the Savior that God has promised.

One day, the angel Gabriel comes to her home in Nazareth. God sends him.

Hail Mary, full of grace, the Lord is with you!

THE VISITATION

Luke 1:39–56

Before leaving, Gabriel tells Mary that her cousin Elizabeth is also expecting a baby.

So Mary decides to go visit Elizabeth.

After a long trip ...

Elizabeth!

Mary!

Most blessed are you among women, and blessed is the fruit of your womb!

You are surely the mother of the Lord. When I heard your greeting, my baby leaped for joy inside me.

Then Mary bursts out with joy:

My soul proclaims the greatness of the Lord! He has looked with favor on his lowly servant. All generations will call me blessed!

After three months, Mary returns to Nazareth to prepare for the birth of Jesus.

THE ANNOUNCEMENT TO JOSEPH

Matthew 1:18–24

In Nazareth, Mary and Joseph get engaged.

Joseph sees that Mary is pregnant, although they do not yet live together.

He cannot understand. He decides not to go through with the marriage.

But while he is asleep, the angel of the Lord appears to him.

Joseph, son of David, do not be afraid to marry Mary! The baby she is expecting comes from the Holy Spirit.

She will give birth to a son, and you will name him Jesus. He is the one who will save his people from their sins.

Joseph does what the angel says: he marries Mary and welcomes her into his home.

THE BIRTH OF JESUS

Luke 2:1–20

The emperor orders a census to count all the people. So Joseph sets out for Bethlehem, the town of David, his ancestor, to be registered with Mary.

When they arrive in Bethlehem, the time comes for Mary to have her baby.

Since there is no room for them at the inn, Joseph and Mary have to take shelter in a stable.

There Mary gives birth to Jesus.

She wraps him up and lays him in a manger.

A little way off, shepherds are in the fields.

Suddenly, the angel of the Lord appears to them.

I proclaim to you good news of great joy. Today a Savior has been born for you. You will find him in Bethlehem, lying in a manger.

The shepherds run to the stable.

There they find Mary and Joseph and the newborn baby in the manger.

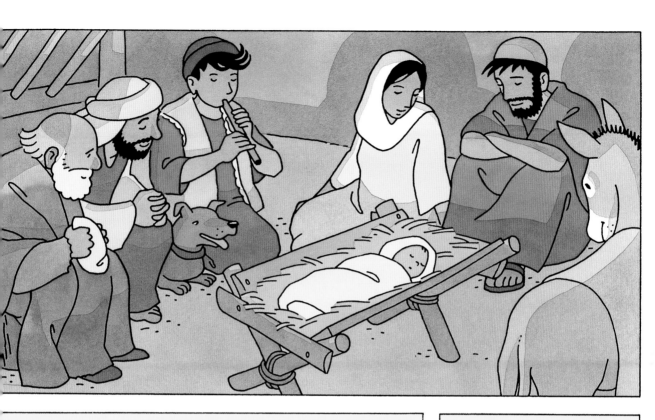

When they tell people what the angel has said, everyone is amazed.

Then they leave, praising God for all they have heard and seen.

THE VISIT OF THE MAGI

Matthew 2:1–12

When Jesus is born in Bethlehem, Judea is ruled by King Herod the Great.

One day, some wise men come to Jerusalem from the East.

Where is the newborn king of the Jews?

We saw his star rising and have come to bow down before him.

King Herod hears of this and is worried.

Who is this king?

Maybe it's the promised Messiah?

Herod calls the priests and scholars.

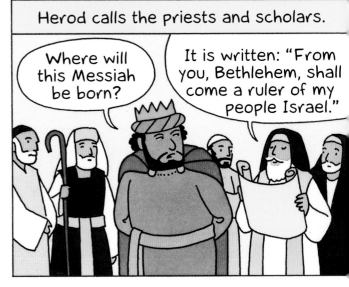

Where will this Messiah be born?

It is written: "From you, Bethlehem, shall come a ruler of my people Israel."

So Herod calls the Magi to him in private.

The child you are looking for is in the region of Bethlehem ...

When you find him, let me know! Then I can go and bow down before him, too.

The Magi set out. And the star goes ahead of them and stops over the place where Jesus is.

They go in and bow down before him. They offer him gifts of gold, frankincense, and myrrh.

But then they are warned in a dream not to go back to Herod, so they return to their country by another way.

THE PRESENTATION OF JESUS IN THE TEMPLE

Luke 2:22–33

Forty days after the birth of Jesus, his parents go to the Temple in Jerusalem. According to the law, they present their son to the Lord and offer the sacrifice made by poor people: two turtledoves.

An old man named Simeon is waiting for the Savior. The Holy Spirit has revealed to him that he will not die until he has seen the Christ. This day, the Spirit leads him to the Temple.

He recognizes Jesus ...

and takes him in his arms.

THE HOLY FAMILY IN NAZARETH

Luke 2:39–40

Mary, Joseph, and Jesus return to Nazareth.

Joseph is a carpenter. He works with wood.

Mary draws water from the well; she keeps the house clean and fixes the meals.

Jesus grows up, and he is filled with wisdom ...

And the grace of God is with him.

JESUS IS LOST AND FOUND

Luke 2:41–51

When Jesus is twelve, he goes on pilgrimage with his parents to Jerusalem for the feast of Passover.

After the feast, the pilgrims travel home.

Where is Jesus?

He must be with friends.

That evening, Mary and Joseph look for Jesus everywhere.

Have you seen our son?

No!

We don't know where he is!

Let's go back to Jerusalem!

At last, three days later, they find him in the Temple, sitting among the teachers of the law.

Jesus!

Son, why have you done this to us?

Why were you looking for me? Did you not know that I had to be in my Father's house?

Jesus goes back to Nazareth with his parents and is obedient to them.

THE BAPTISM OF JESUS

Matthew 3:1–17

In the desert, John is announcing the coming of Jesus.

Change your heart, for the kingdom of heaven is at hand!

Many come to be baptized by him in the waters of the Jordan River.

I baptize you with water, but the one who is coming after me will baptize you with the Holy Spirit!

Jesus comes from Galilee to the banks of the Jordan.

He asks John to baptize him, but John does not dare.

I need to be baptized by you, and yet you are coming to me?

This is how it must be ...

After being baptized, Jesus rises up from the water and, behold, he sees the Spirit of God coming down like a dove over him ...

... as a voice from the heavens proclaims:

This is my beloved Son, with whom I am well pleased!

JESUS IN THE DESERT

Matthew 4:1–11

After his baptism, Jesus leaves for the desert, led by the Holy Spirit.

He goes without food for forty days.

Then the tempter approaches ...

If you are the Son of God, command that these stones become loaves of bread!

No! It is written: "Man does not live by bread alone, but by the word of God!"

Then the devil takes him to Jerusalem right to the top of the Temple.

If you are the Son of God, jump! God will send his angels to catch you!

No! It is written: "You shall not put the Lord, your God, to the test."

Then the devil takes him to the top of a very high mountain.

I will give you all this if you will bow down and worship me.

Get away, Satan! It is written: "You shall worship the Lord, your God, and him alone shall you serve!"

Then the devil leaves him, and angels come to Jesus to serve him.

AT THE SYNAGOGUE IN NAZARETH

Luke 4:16–22

After his stay in the desert, Jesus returns to Nazareth, where he grew up.

On the Sabbath day, he enters the synagogue.

He gets up to do the reading and is handed the Book of the Prophet Isaiah.

Unrolling the scroll, he finds the place where it is written:

The Spirit of the Lord is upon me, because he has anointed me to bring glad tidings to the poor ...

After the reading, Jesus sits. Everyone stares at him.

Today, this Scripture passage you have just heard has come true.

And everyone is amazed at the gracious words he speaks ...

COME AND YOU WILL SEE

John 1:35–42

John the Baptist is sitting with two of his disciples. He points to Jesus walking by.

Behold, the Lamb of God.

What do you seek?

Master, where are you staying?

Come and see!

And they stay with him that day.

One of them, Andrew, goes to find his brother Simon.

We have found the Messiah!

You are Simon, the son of John; you will be called Peter.

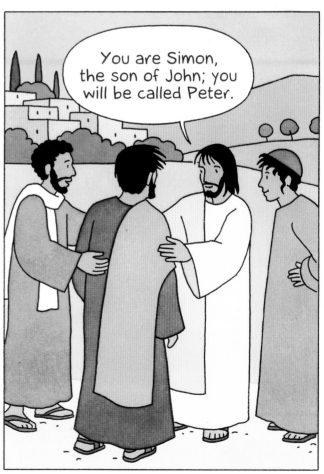

THE CHOICE OF THE TWELVE APOSTLES

Luke 6:12–16

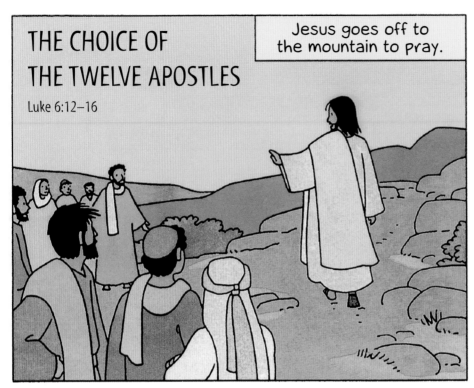

Jesus goes off to the mountain to pray.

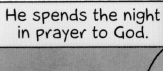 He spends the night in prayer to God.

Morning comes.

Gather round me!

Simon ...

NICODEMUS

John 3:1–8

A Pharisee comes to see Jesus at night. It is Nicodemus, an important leader of the Jews.

Master, we know very well that God has sent you to teach us ...

No one can do what you do unless God is with him!

Amen, I say to you, no one can see the kingdom of God without being born anew.

How can an old person be born anew? Can he go back inside of his mother to be born a second time?

Amen, I say to you, no one can enter the kingdom of God without being born of water and the Spirit.

You were born from your mother, but you must also be born from the Spirit!

You hear wind, but you don't know where it comes from or where it's going!

It's like that for everyone who is born by the breath of the Spirit ...

THE BEATITUDES

Matthew 5:1–12

When Jesus sees the crowd, he goes up the mountain. He sits down; his disciples gather around him. Then he begins to teach them ...

Blessed are the poor in spirit: theirs is the kingdom of heaven! Blessed they who mourn: they will be comforted!

Blessed the meek: they will inherit the land! Blessed they who hunger and thirst for righteousness: they will be satisfied!

Blessed the merciful: they will obtain mercy! Blessed the pure of heart: they will see God!

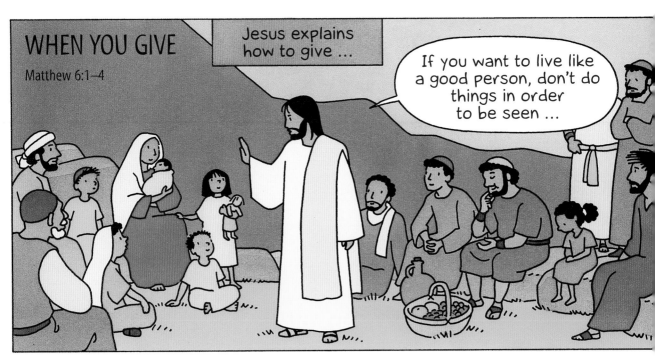

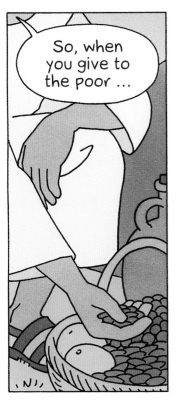

WHEN YOU PRAY

Matthew 6:5–6

When you pray, don't be like people who like to show off ...

They like to stand up in the synagogues and on street corners so that everyone will see them.

They have already received their reward!

THE STORM IS CALMED

Matthew 8:23–27

Jesus gets into the boat with his disciples.

A big storm blows up. Soon the boat is filling with water.

All the while, Jesus sleeps.

Lord, save us!

Why are you afraid?

Jesus gets up and yells at the wind and the sea:

Quiet! Be still!

And right away there is a great calm ...

Who is this, that even the wind and the sea obey him?

LORD, TEACH US HOW TO PRAY

Luke 11:1–4
Matthew 6:9–13

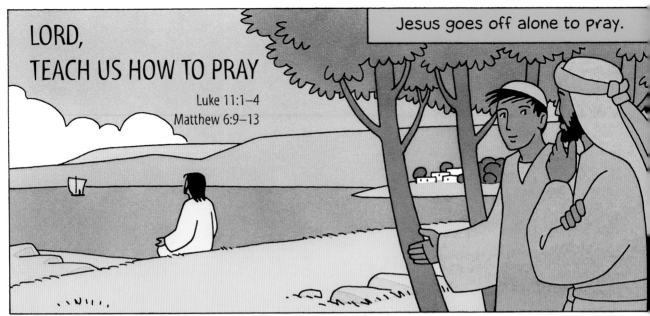

Jesus goes off alone to pray.

When he has finished ...

Lord, teach us how to pray!

When you pray, say ...

THE SOWER

Mark 4:1–9

Jesus is teaching by the shore of the lake. Such a big crowd gathers that he gets into a boat. He tells them a parable to help them understand how to receive the word of God.

Listen!

A sower goes out to plant seeds ...

Some seed falls by the roadside, and the birds come and eat it up.

SENT ON A MISSION

Mark 6:7–13; 30–34

Jesus gathers his apostles. For the first time, he is going to send them off on a mission.

Take nothing with you!

Take no bread, no bag, no money, no change of clothes.

Wherever you are welcomed, stay there until you leave that place.

The apostles go out, two by two ...

Repent!

They chase away many demons ...

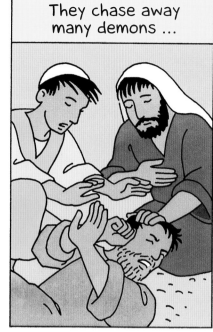

They heal the sick ...

When they return, they tell Jesus everything they have done and taught.

Come, rest awhile!

Pray that the master of the harvest will send out workers for his harvest!

Go ahead! I am sending you like lambs among wolves ...

Take no money, no bag, no change of sandals ...

Don't lose any time talking to people along the road ...

Wherever you go in, first say: "Peace be to this house!"

And Jesus sends them off two by two.

THE MUSTARD SEED

Matthew 13:31–32

Jesus wants to help us discover the kingdom of God.

So he tells a parable:

The kingdom of God is like a mustard seed …

… that a man took and planted in a field.

The mustard seed is the smallest of seeds.

But it grows into the largest of plants.

WHO DO YOU SAY THAT I AM?

Mark 8:27–30

Jesus travels with his disciples.

As they walk, he asks them:

Who do people say that I am?

Some say you are John the Baptist.

Others say you are Elijah …

Or one of the prophets.

And what about you? Who do you say that I am?

It is Peter who answers:

You are the Messiah!

Then Jesus orders them not to tell anyone about him.

WHO IS THE GREATEST?

Mark 9:33–37

Jesus and his disciples travel across Galilee.

They arrive in Capernaum.

What were you arguing about on the way here?

The disciples do not dare answer, for they had been arguing about which of them was the greatest.

THE SAMARITAN WOMAN

John 4:4–14

Jesus and his disciples cross Samaria and arrive at Jacob's well near the town of Sychar.

The disciples go off to buy food. Jesus sits down to wait for them. He is tired from the journey.

A Samaritan woman comes to the well for water.

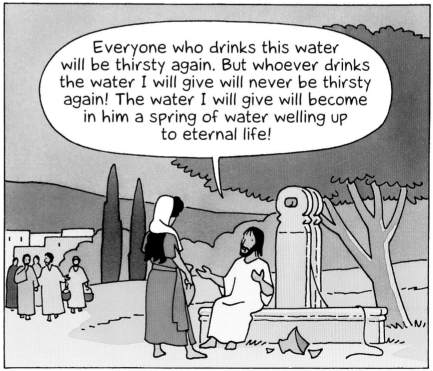

THE MULTIPLICATION OF THE LOAVES

John 6:1–13

A big crowd gathers around Jesus on a hillside near Lake Tiberias ...

Where can we buy bread for them to eat?

We'll never find enough bread to feed all these people!

This boy has five loaves of bread and two fish ... but that's not much!

Have everyone sit down!

Jesus takes the bread, gives thanks, and has them pass it around with the fish.

Everyone has as much as he can eat!

When everyone is full ...

Gather up the leftovers so that nothing is wasted.

And the disciples fill twelve baskets!

THE BREAD OF LIFE

John 6:22-60

The day after the multiplication of the loaves, the crowd sees that Jesus has left.

So the people get into their boats to go look for him.

They find Jesus on the other side of the lake.

Master, when did you get here?

You are looking for me because I gave you some food!

But the bread of God comes down from heaven and gives life to the world.

Lord, give us this bread always!

I am the bread of life.

Whoever comes to me will never be hungry. I came down from heaven to do the will of the one who sent me.

We know his father and his mother. How can he say: "I came down from heaven"?

Stop murmuring! I am the living bread that came down from heaven. The bread I will give is my flesh for the life of the world!

Eat his flesh?! Who can listen to him anymore?

And many of his disciples quit following him. Jesus turns to Peter and the apostles:

Do you want to leave, too?

Master, to whom would we go? It is you who have the words of eternal life!

65

THE TRANSFIGURATION

Luke 9:28–36

Jesus goes up the mountain to pray with Peter, James, and John.

While he is praying, his face changes completely and his clothes become dazzling white. And two men are speaking with him: Moses and Elijah have appeared in glory!

But the three disciples have fallen asleep.

When they wake up, they see Jesus in his glory and the two men beside him.

Master, I ... I'll put up three tents, for you, for Moses, and for Elijah.

Peter does not know what he is saying!

And at that moment:

THIS IS MY SON, MY CHOSEN ONE; LISTEN TO HIM!

When the voice stops speaking, the disciples see only Jesus alone.

They go back down the mountain, and the disciples tell no one about what they have seen.

JESUS AND THE CHILDREN

Mark 10:13–16

People bring their little children to Jesus so that he might touch them.

But the disciples push them away.

When Jesus sees this, he gets angry.

Let the children come to me!

Don't stop them, because the kingdom of God belongs to ones like them.

Whoever does not accept the kingdom of God like a child will not enter it!

And he blesses the children.

MARTHA AND MARY

Luke 10:38–42

Jesus arrives in a village. A woman named Martha welcomes him into her house.

Martha has a sister named Mary.

Martha is very busy serving. As for Mary, she sits at the Lord's feet listening to him.

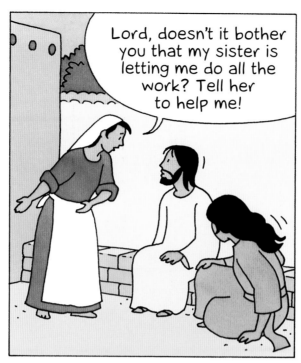

Lord, doesn't it bother you that my sister is letting me do all the work? Tell her to help me!

Martha, Martha! You're busy and worried about many things ...

But only one thing is necessary.

Mary chose the better part; it will not be taken away from her!

THE RICH MAN

Mark 10:17–22

A man comes up to Jesus and asks him a question:

Master, what must I do to have eternal life?

If you want eternal life, obey the commandments.

Master, I have obeyed all of them since I was little!

Then Jesus looks at him with love.

You still need one thing …

Go and sell all that you have and give to the poor, and you will have treasure in heaven. Then come, follow me.

Hearing these words, the man goes away sad because he has many riches.

How hard it is for those who have riches to enter the kingdom of God!

THE POOR WIDOW'S CONTRIBUTION

Mark 12:41–44

One day, in the Temple of Jerusalem ...

Jesus sits facing the treasury.

He watches the people putting in their contribution.

Many rich people give lots of money.

A widow arrives. She is poor.

She gives just two small coins.

Jesus tells his friends:

This poor widow gave more than all the others, because she gave all that she had ...

She gave everything!

THE WOMAN WHO SINNED

John 8:1–11

A big crowd has come to the Temple of Jerusalem to listen to Jesus. The scribes and the Pharisees bring a woman before him ...

Master, this woman was caught in the act of doing something evil!

The law of Moses says that we must kill women like this by stoning them. What do you say?

Jesus bends down and writes on the ground.

Are you going to answer?

Whoever among you is without sin, let him throw the first stone ...

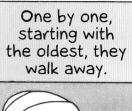

One by one, starting with the oldest, they walk away.

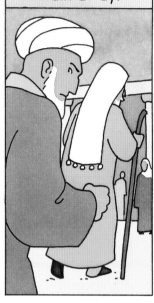

Woman, where are they all? Has no one condemned you?

No one, Lord.

Nor do I condemn you. Go, and don't sin anymore!

THE PRODIGAL SON

Luke 15:11–24

Jesus explains how God our Father forgives us.

A man has two sons ...

The younger one asks for his inheritance.

Then he leaves for a faraway land ...

... where he wastes all his money.

When he has nothing left, he gets a job taking care of pigs.

I'm starving! I'm going to return to my father's house.

So he sets off on his way home to his father.

His father spots him in the distance.

Father, I've sinned against heaven and against you. I don't deserve to be called your son!

But the father is so happy to have his son back, he arranges a big celebration.

ZACCHAEUS

Luke 19:1–10

Jesus arrives in Jericho. Zacchaeus, a rich but not very honest man, would really like to see him.

But how can he? Zacchaeus is too short!

So he runs ahead and climbs up a sycamore tree.

When Jesus arrives, he looks up at Zacchaeus.

Zacchaeus, come down, for today I want to stay at your house!

He comes down fast.

He welcomes Jesus with great joy.

He's gone to see that thief!

Because Jesus loves him, Zacchaeus decides to change his ways:

Yes, Lord, I will give half of what I own to the poor, and if I've cheated anyone, I will pay him back four times more!

Today, salvation has come to this house! I came to search out and to save what was lost.

THE ENTRY INTO JERUSALEM

Mark 11:1–10

A few days before the feast of Passover, Jesus and his disciples are getting close to Jerusalem.

Here's the village of Bethphage!

Go ahead!

You'll find a little donkey there. Untie it and bring it to me.

Why are you untying that donkey?

The Master needs it.

He'll send it right back to you!

The disciples put their coats on the donkey's back and take it to Jesus.

Many people cover the road with their coats and with branches.

Hosanna!

Blessed is he who comes in the name of the Lord!

Long live the Son of David!

Hosanna in the highest!

THE TWO COMMANDMENTS

Mark 12:28–34

In the Temple, the priests and the scholars ask Jesus all kinds of questions. A scribe is listening nearby …

He answers well! I'll ask him something, too.

What is the first of all the commandments?

This is the first: "Hear, O Israel, the Lord our God is the only God … "

"You shall love the Lord your God with all your heart, with all your soul, with all your mind, and with all your strength." The second one is like it: "You shall love your neighbor as yourself."

There is no other commandment greater than these.

Well said, Master!

To love God and one's neighbor is worth more than any offering or sacrifice!

You are not far from the kingdom of God.

Jesus speaks to the Pharisees and says:

THE GOOD SHEPHERD

John 10:1–5 and 11–16

I am the good shepherd.

Anyone who gets into the sheepfold without going through the gate is a robber.

The one who enters through the gate is the shepherd. The sheep listen to him.

He calls each sheep by name.

They follow him because they know his voice.

They will never follow a stranger; they'll run away from him!

I am the good shepherd. I know my sheep, and my sheep know me. I give my life for my sheep.

I have other sheep that don't belong to this sheepfold. I have to lead them, too. They will listen to my voice: there will be just one flock and one shepherd.

THE SUPPER
IN BETHANY

Matthew 26:6–13

A few days before his death on the cross, Jesus is invited to Simon's house in Bethany.

During the meal, a woman enters ...

She has a bottle of very expensive perfume, which she pours on Jesus' head.

What a waste!

We could have sold it for a lot of money ...

... and given it to the poor as a good deed!

Why are you upsetting her?

She has done a good deed for me.

You will always have poor people around you! But you won't always have me.

By perfuming me, she has prepared my body for the tomb.

Yes, wherever this Gospel is preached, people will remember her and what she has done.

THE LAST SUPPER

Mark 14:12–26
John 13:1–14

Jesus is in Jerusalem at the time of Passover.

Where would you like us to prepare your Passover meal?

Go into the city. There you'll find a man carrying a jug of water. Follow him ...

Where is the room for the Passover meal?

That evening, when everything is ready, Jesus arrives with the twelve apostles.

Knowing he is about to die, Jesus shows his friends how much he loves them right to the very end.

During supper, Jesus takes some bread, blesses it, and gives it to his apostles.

Take and eat: this is my body.

Then he takes a cup filled with wine.

Take and drink: this is my blood.

Do this in memory of me.

After they sing a psalm, they leave for the Mount of Olives.

JESUS GIVES HIS LIFE FOR US

Matthew 26:36–67 and 27

In the garden of Gethsemane, the disciples fall asleep while Jesus prays.

Father, ... may your will be done ...

Soon some soldiers arrive and take Jesus prisoner.

Jewish and Roman leaders condemn him to death.

Crucify him!

They hit him and make fun of him. And he takes it all.

He has to carry his own cross to the hill of Golgotha.

Jesus is nailed to the cross and gives up his life for us.

That evening, his friends place his body in a tomb.

THE RESURRECTION OF JESUS

Matthew 28:1–8
Luke 24:13–35
Mark 16:1–7
John 20:19–29

On the third day after Jesus dies, some women come to the tomb.

But when they get there, they see that the stone has already been rolled away.

And the angel of the Lord appears.

Don't be afraid!

Jesus isn't here anymore. He has risen as he said! Quick, go tell his disciples!

Frightened but overjoyed, they run to bring the news to the disciples.

And, well ... all this happened three days ago, but this morning some of the women in our group went to the tomb. It was empty, and they couldn't find his body ...

They even talked about a vision: an angel, who said that Jesus was alive! Our friends went to see, and they couldn't find him either ...

So you haven't understood! How slow your hearts are to believe what the prophets said ...

And Jesus explains the Scriptures to them.

So you see, the Messiah had to go through all that.

Later ...

We've arrived!

I'm going farther.

No, stay with us! It's getting dark.

While they eat supper, Jesus takes bread, blesses it, and gives it to them.

Then their eyes are opened!

It's you, Lord!

But Jesus has disappeared.

Wasn't your heart on fire when he talked to us along the road?

Quick, let's get back to Jerusalem!

There they find the eleven apostles and their friends.

Jesus is truly risen!

He appeared to Peter!

And to us, too! He walked along with us ...

And we recognized him when he broke the bread!

One disciple was not there—Thomas.

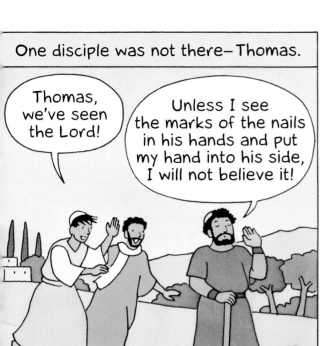

Thomas, we've seen the Lord!

Unless I see the marks of the nails in his hands and put my hand into his side, I will not believe it!

A week later ...

Peace be with you!

Thomas, put your finger here, see my hands.

Stretch out your hand, see my side.

My Lord and my God!

Blessed those who believe without seeing!

PETER, DO YOU LOVE ME?

John 21:1–17

Some time after the resurrection of Jesus, Peter, and some other friends of Jesus go fishing. They try all night, but catch nothing.

Suddenly …

Cast the net to the right of the boat!

They cast the net, and there are so many fish, they cannot even pull in the net!

Then, they recognize Jesus. Very happy, they hurry to shore and have breakfast with him.

THE ASCENSION

Luke 24:50–53
Acts of the Apostles 1:8–12

Jesus leads his disciples near Bethany.

You are going to receive power when the Holy Spirit comes upon you.

Then you will be my witnesses in Jerusalem, all over Judea and Samaria, right to the ends of the earth.

He raises his hands and blesses them.

As he blesses them, he leaves them and is carried up to heaven.

Men of Galilee, why are you standing there looking up at the sky?

Jesus who has been taken up from you will come back the same way you saw him going away ...

The disciples return to Jerusalem full of joy.

PENTECOST

Acts of the Apostles 2:1–41

In Jerusalem on the feast of Pentecost, the apostles gather with Mary and other friends of Jesus.

Suddenly, they hear a sound like a gust of wind. They see what looks like tongues of fire settling on each of them.

Filled with the Holy Spirit, they begin to speak in different languages.

Alleluia!

Glory to you, Lord!

Hearing the noise, a crowd gathers. Many are from foreign lands. Yet each hears the disciples speak of the wonders of God in his own language!

God has raised Jesus of Nazareth from the dead!

Everyone is amazed. That day, three thousand people ask to be baptized. And that is the first Christian community.